Pi

FISHING STEP BY STEP

Pike

with

Barrie Rickards

CASSELL
LONDON

CASSELL & COMPANY LIMITED
35 Red Lion Square, London WC1R 4SG
and at Sydney, Auckland, Toronto, Johannesburg,
an affiliate of
Macmillan Publishing Co., Inc.,
New York.

First published 1976

ISBN 0 304 29747 X

Printed by Ian Allan Printing Ltd.

INTRODUCTION

If you can put a rod together, use a reel and handle a landing net, then these books are your next need. With this series of books the angler is given the chance of seeing just how the expert goes about catching the fish that have made his name a household word in the world of fishing.

Peter Mohan has used his unique knowledge of angling personalities to select the right angler for each book, and then edited the series as a whole.

Ken Whitehead has spent days at the water with the experts, patiently filming and planning every photograph so that each picture shows in detail where, when and how the many tasks are approached.

Study the pictures and compare your methods, your tackle and your whole approach to fishing. This is how you will gain the confidence that brings success.

Whilst the books in themselves are interesting to read, they are also a programmed technique that is progressive. With careful study the new angler, or one wishing to improve his angling, will learn how each skill at the water should be tackled, and by re-reading he will be able to adopt the expert's way of tackling every situation.

2

1 Thirty pounders cannot, at present, be separated from twenty pounders by angling techniques; but if this book helps one step towards such great captures the authors will be happy.

2 This stepped-up carp rod by Olivers of Knebworth cast a mackerel head a long way to catch the 31½ pounder. The rod action is powerful but slow and is ideal for casting half a mackerel 70 yards on 12lb breaking strain line. At the same time it is a nice tool on which to play even quite small pike.

3

4

5

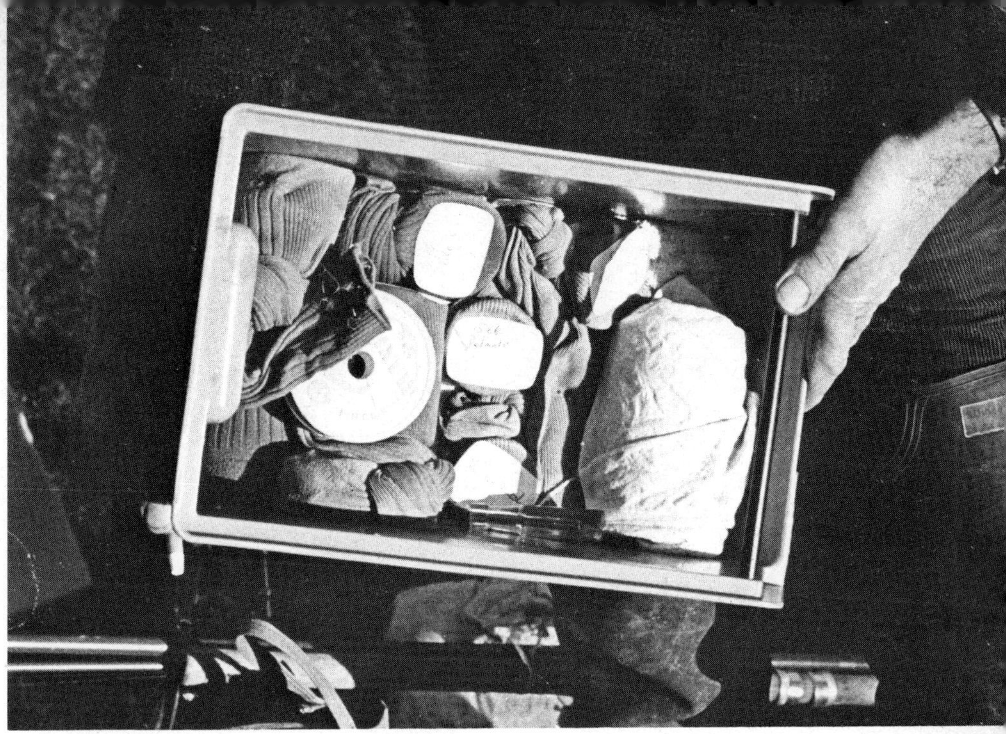

6

3 The rods I normally use for livebaiting are a Davenport and Fordham normal 10 foot carp rod, or a Sportex 10 foot carp rod, both being lighter than the deadbait rods, but still with a soft action rather than a tip action.

4 Several rods of all three types are made up at the very beginning of a day's piking.

5 The reels are Mitchells with clip-on spools and Intrepid Supertwins, also with the same feature.

6 A box with spare reels, spools and line, all carefully labelled, is carried.

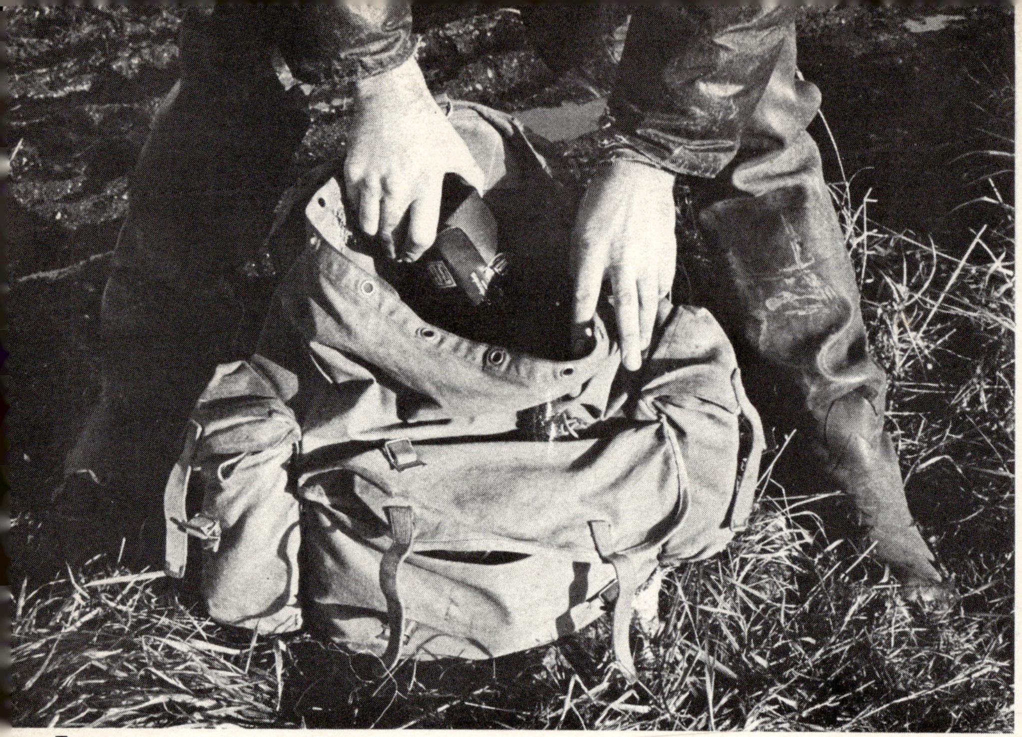

7

8

7 A big rucksack takes everything except livebait, rods and umbrellas.

8 The rucksack contents are varied, and include a barometer . . .

9 There is a snap tackle holder which fits snugly in a dried milk tin.

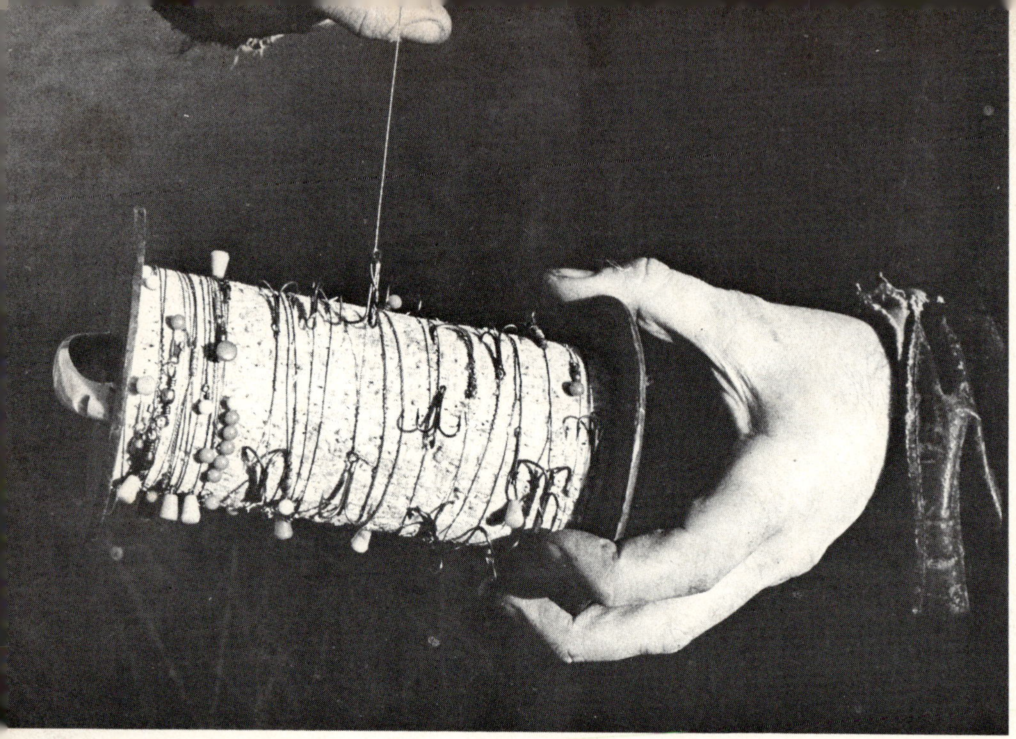

10

11

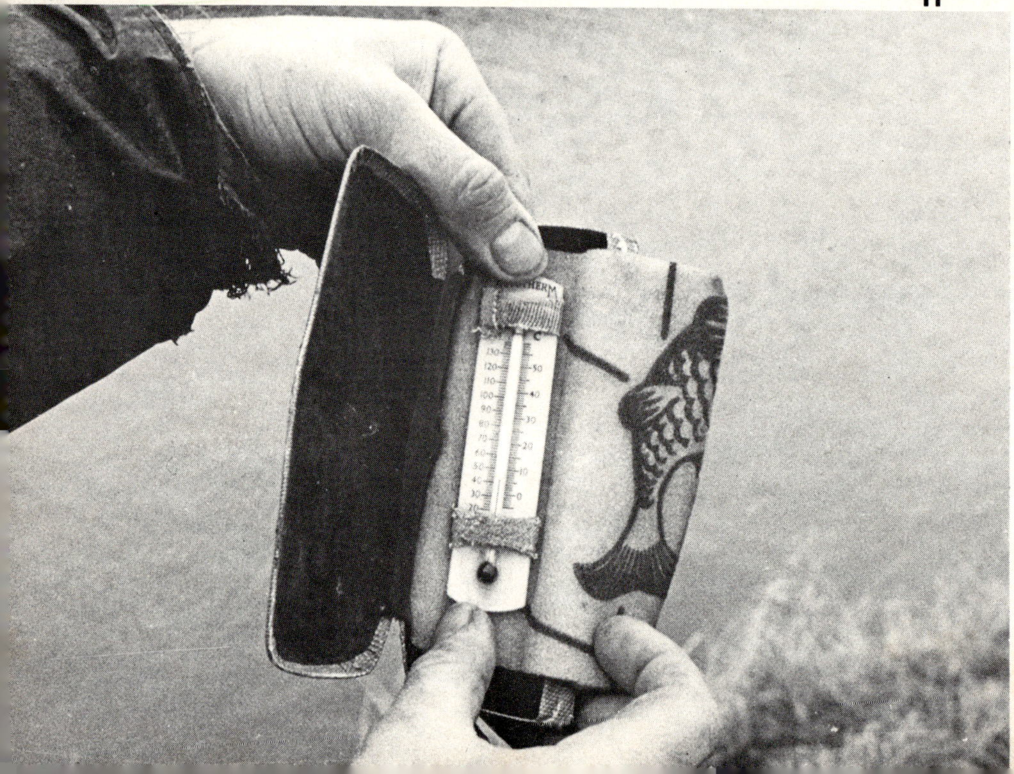

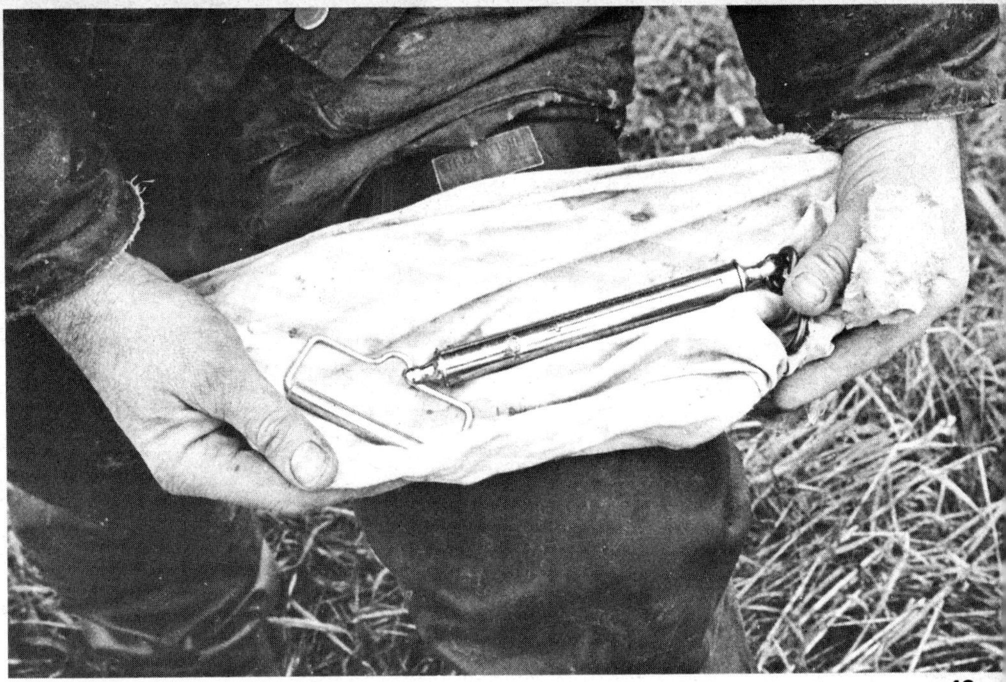

12

10 Snap tackles, traces etc. are held on the balsa log by means of mapping pins.

11 The thermometer fits in a foam-lined spectacle case.

12 The spring balance is always carefully wrapped in a soft, slightly oily, cloth.

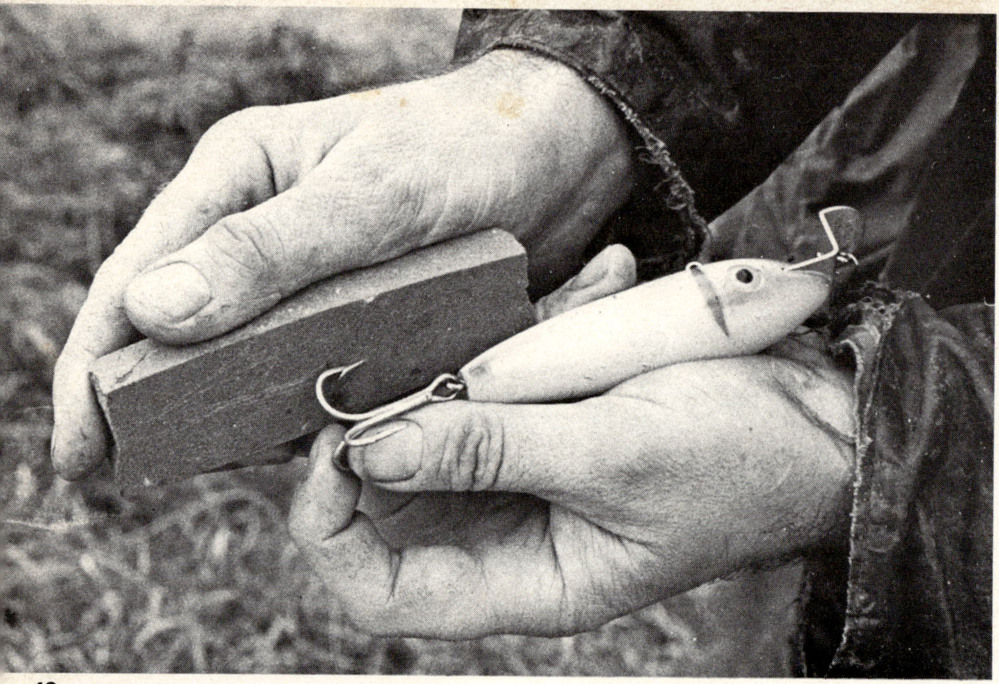

13

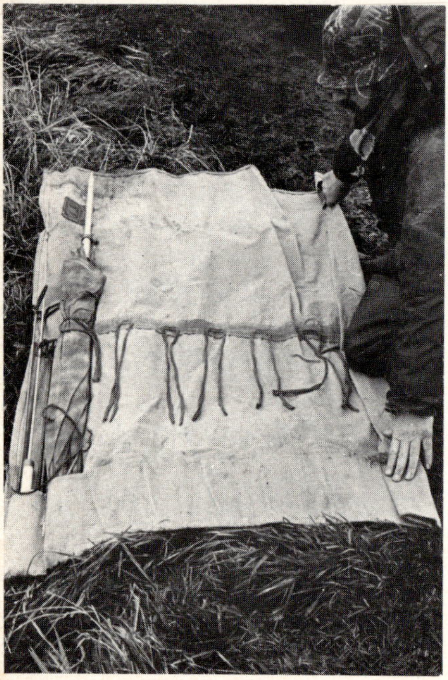

14

15

16

13 A sharpening stone is handy in the big front pocket of the rucksack.

14 Large and long items fit easily into a roll-up rod holdall.

15 A camouflaged umbrella is less likely to frighten fish.

16 Use a spike to anchor a brolly in the winter winds.

17

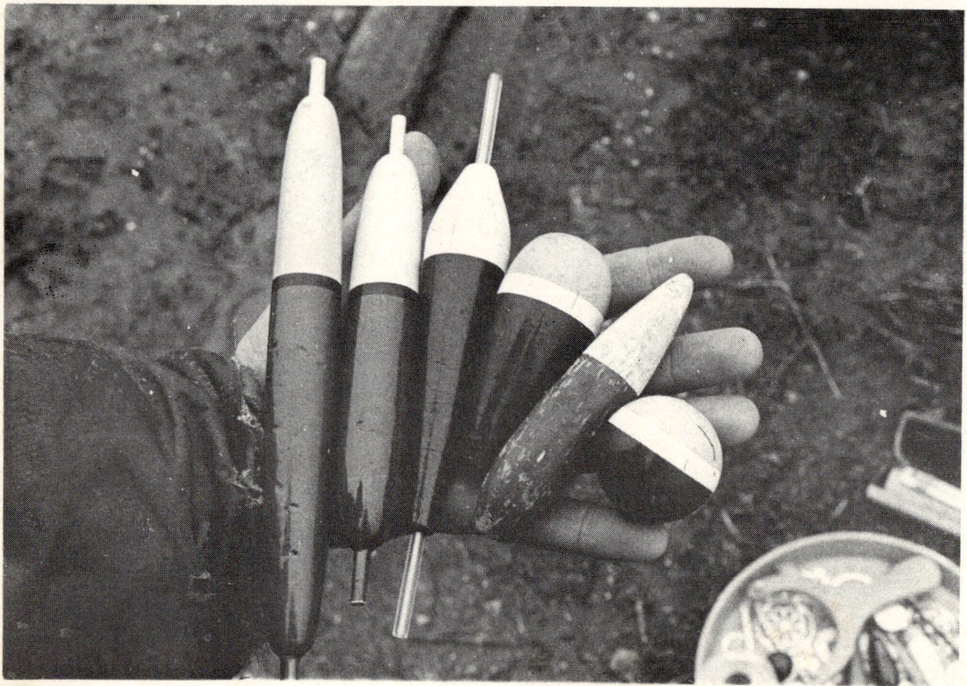
18

19

17 More rucksack front pocket contents: pilchard oil, line grease, bubble float, self-cocking black float, and beads for float stops.

18 A selection of sliding floats, the two on the right being used most often.

19 Side pocket contents. In addition to those already seen, there are a catapult, gag, paternoster line on a bulk spool, Alasticum wire, and a syringe.

NATIONAL DRIED MILK

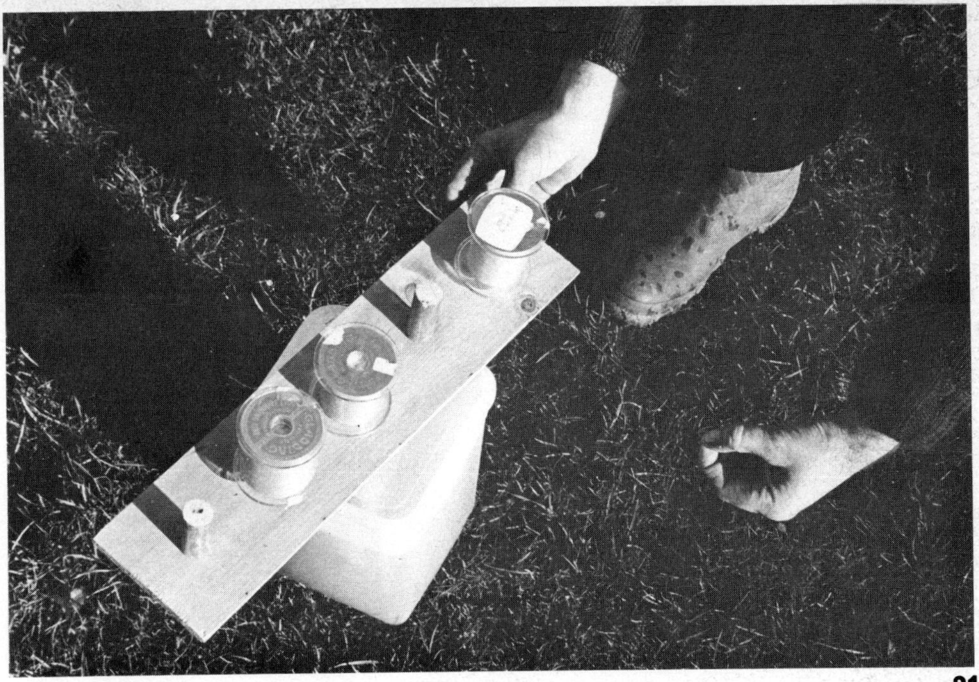

21

20 These are only the small items in the rucksack. In addition to these which include unhooking gear, weighing gear and snap tackle making equipment, are the following items: binoculars, food, soft seat, drink, deadbaits, landing and keepnets, a chair, a camera or two, and so on . . .

21 'Spare' fishing line not carried in the van is stored on bulk spools on a home-made dispenser.

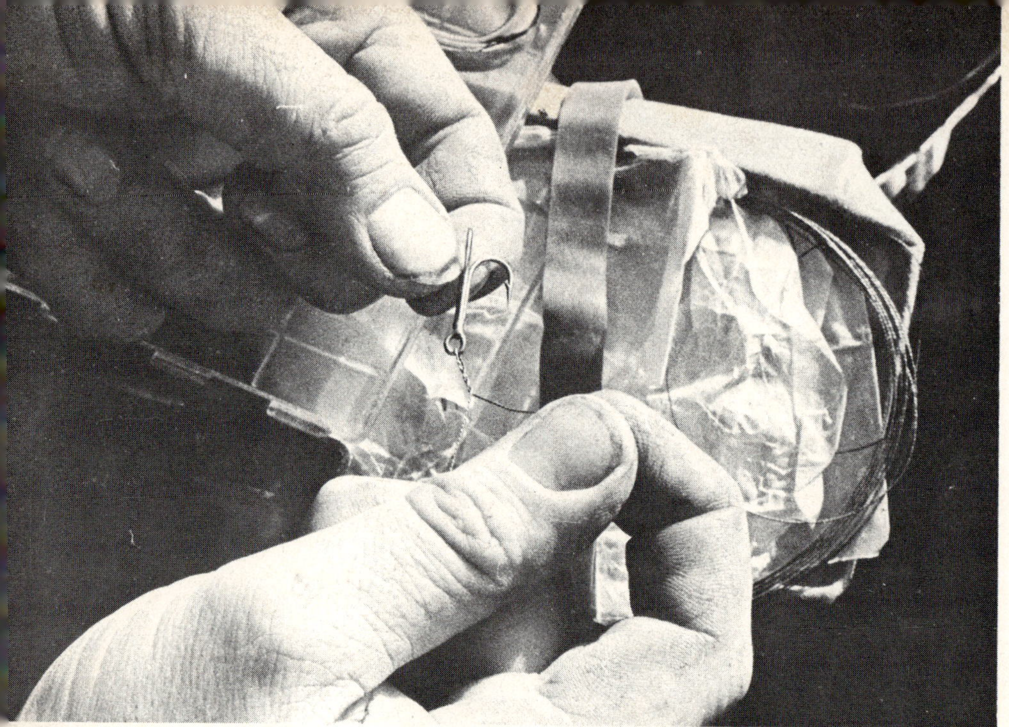

22

23

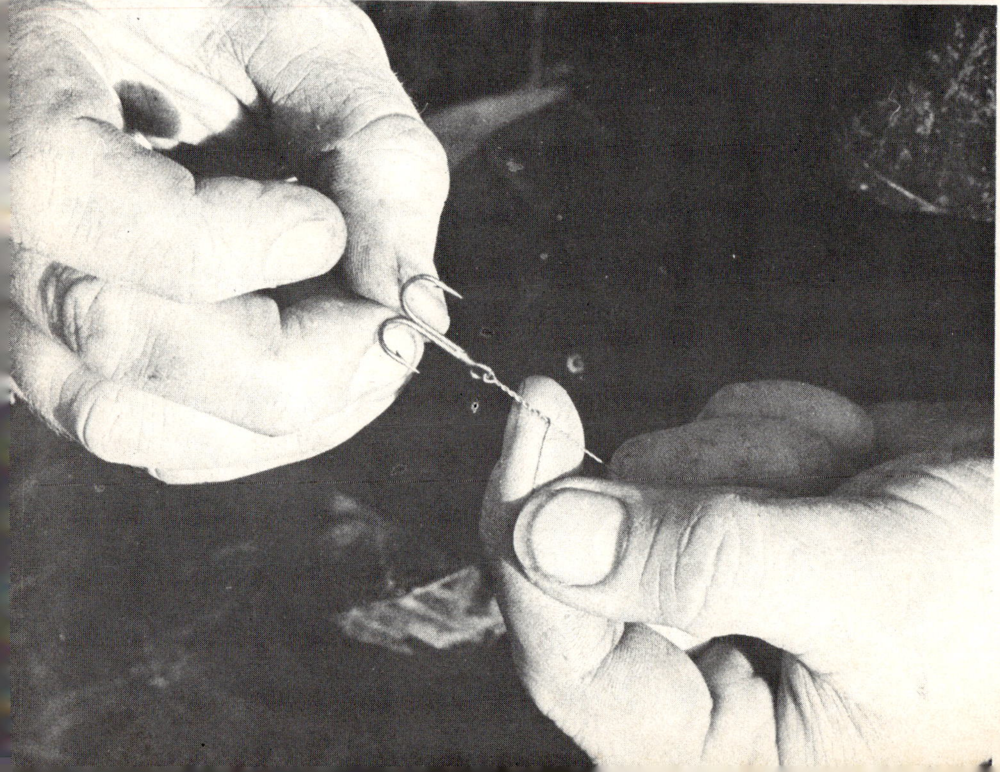

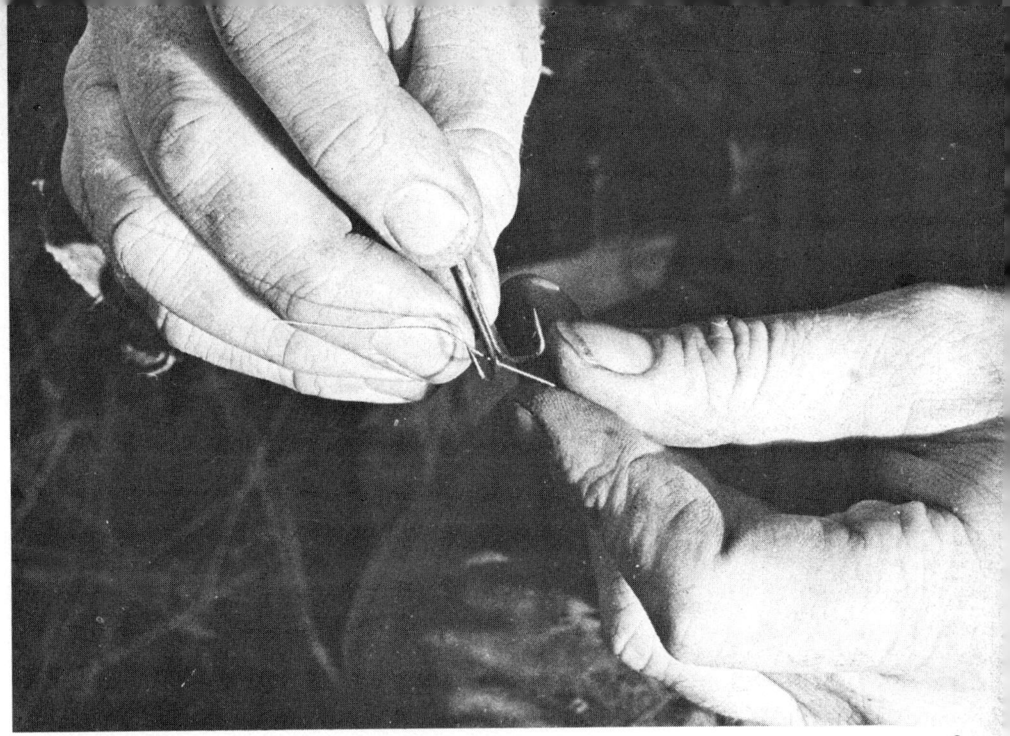

24

22 Beginning to make up a snap tackle rig: selecting small hooks and Alasticum wire.

23 Firstly the ordinary treble is tied to the length of wire simply by twisting an overlapping inch of the wire firmly together.

24 Then a Ryder hook is added on the wire which passes through the lower ring first, then once round the shank before coming out through the top ring or eye.

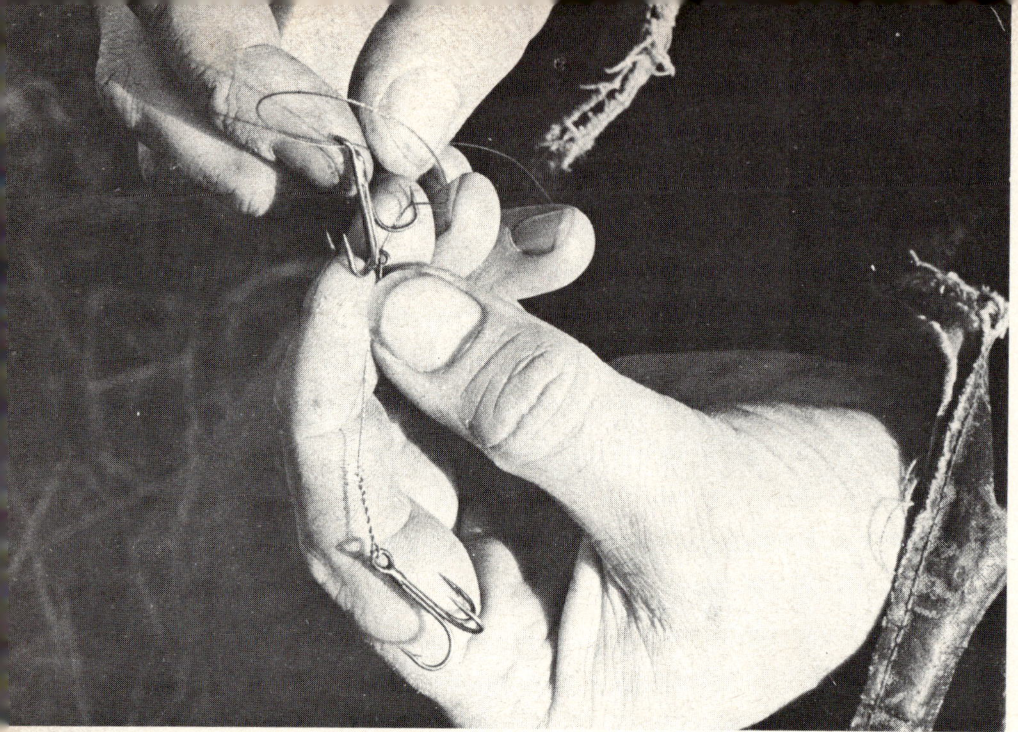

25

26

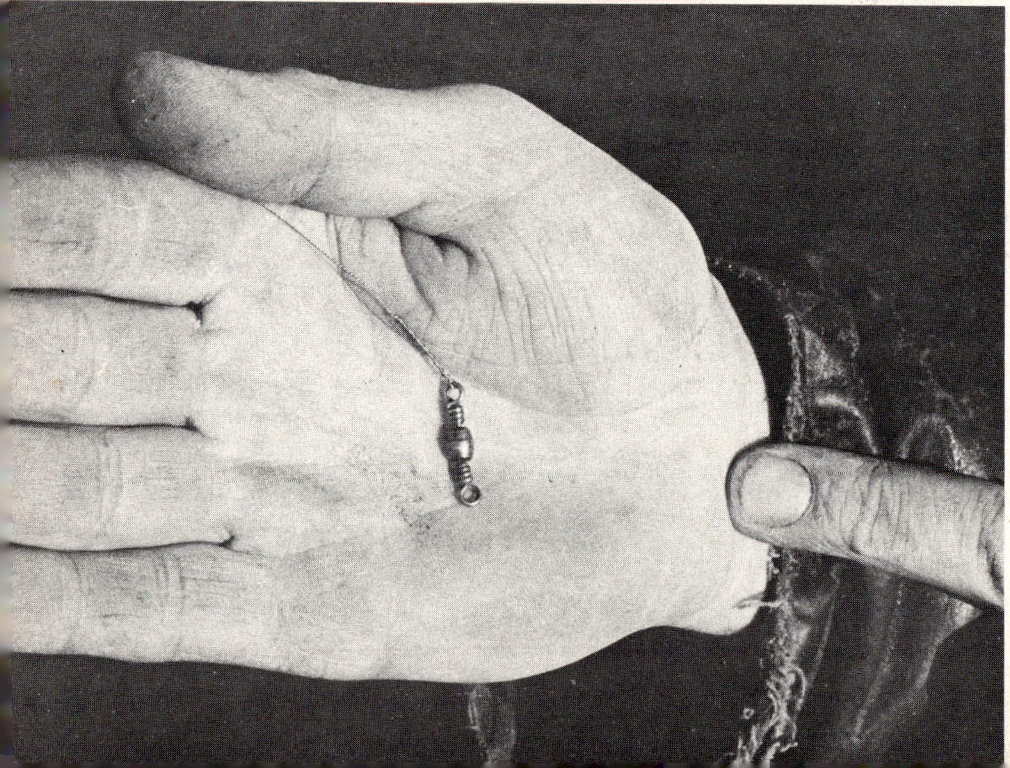

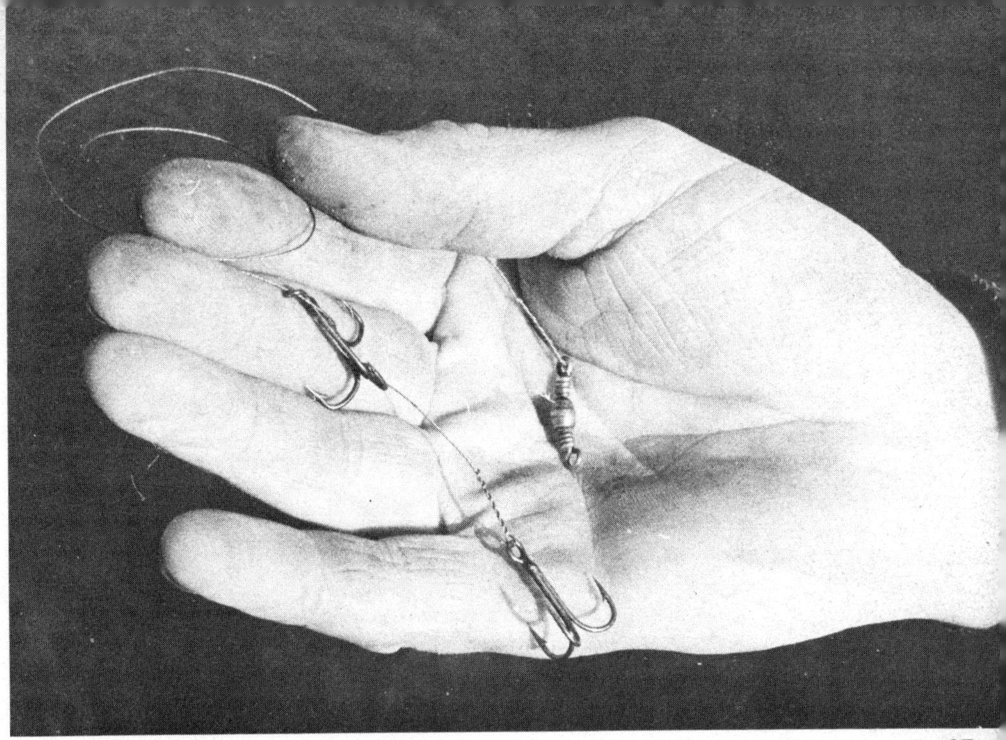

25 The Ryder hook in position.

26 A swivel is attached to the other end of the twelve inches of wire in the same way as the first treble.

27 The completed snap tackle.

28

29

30

28 Now for some bait. Almost everything in the way of deadbaits can be stored for years in a deep freeze.

29 One of the trays from the deep freeze with some of the author's labelled deadbaits: mackerel, herrings, sprats, sardines, bloaters, roach, rudd, dace, etc.

30 Deadbaits can also be kept in a solution of formalin in water, if a deep freeze is not available.

31

32

31 Preparing a mackerel for the deep freeze. First lay on freezer wrapping tissue.

32 Then fold over the tissue, wrapping it close to the fish.

33 The result is like a stick of rock. Indeed if you have no knife they can be snapped in two.

34

35

36

34 Baits can be thawed in water if needs be. In this case a block of sprats is being thawed out since it is usually quite impossible to pull a frozen bait off the block. Large, wrapped baits do not cling together.

35 Livebait stored in a garden pond, in this case in a distilled water container. The wooden plank is for insulation against cold nights.

36 The distilled water container has numerous ½in holes drilled in the sides to allow ample circulation of water.

37

38

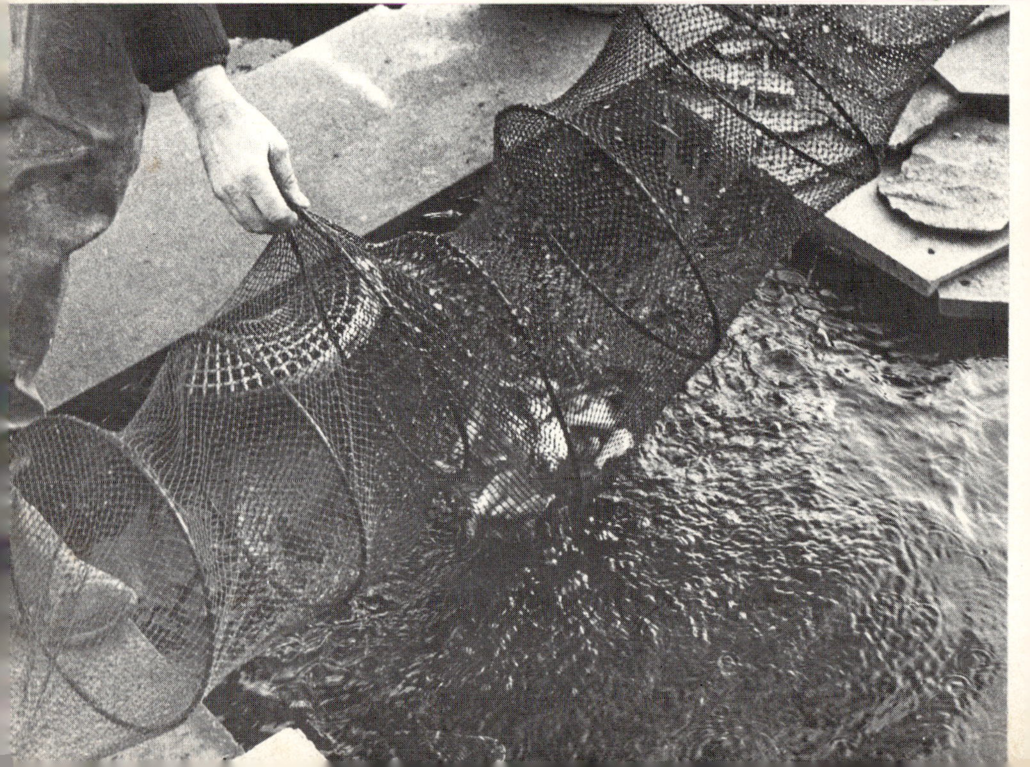

37 A clothes basket is just as good.

38 Garden ponds will also sustain a healthy stock of bait in a sizeable keepnet. Obviously the knotless types are best, although there is little trouble with the normal keepnets.

39 A three-foot-cube wooden box with half inch gaps every six inches is probably the best livebait store of all if placed under a tree and over a gravel bottom. Further insulation is provided by a wooden top and heaped pondweed.

40

41

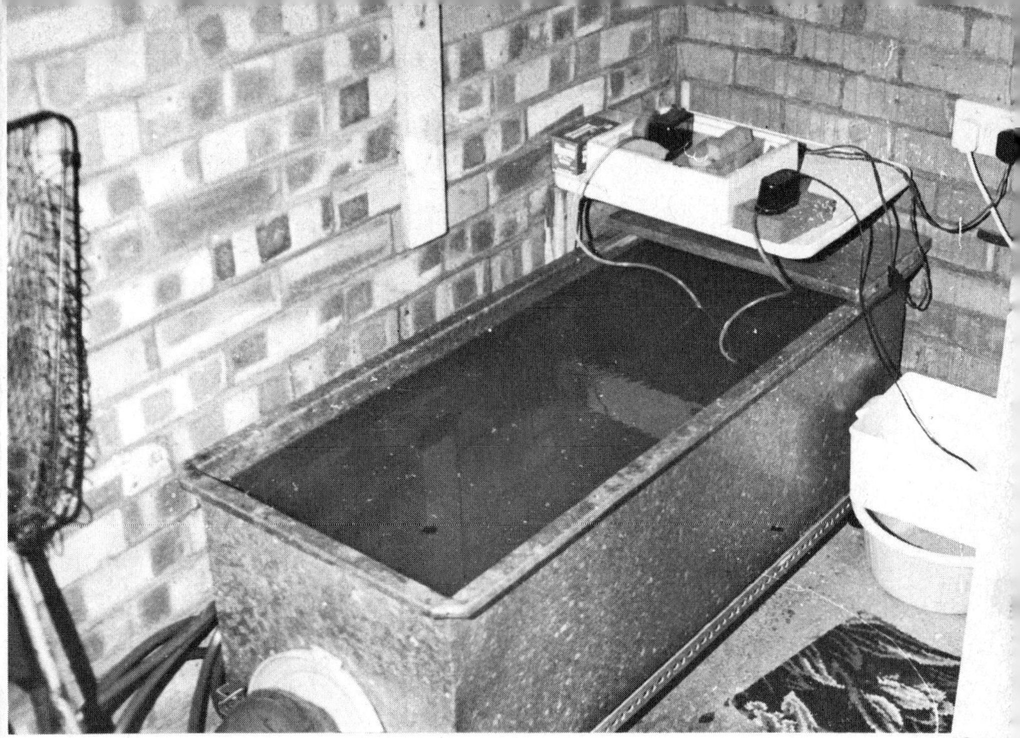

42

40 The lid must also be weighted down with logs as a rule, otherwise it floats.

41 The traditional Norfolk bait box will keep a healthy stock for months on end during the winter.

42 A horse trough, on a trolley, with aerators in position is convenient storage for bait.

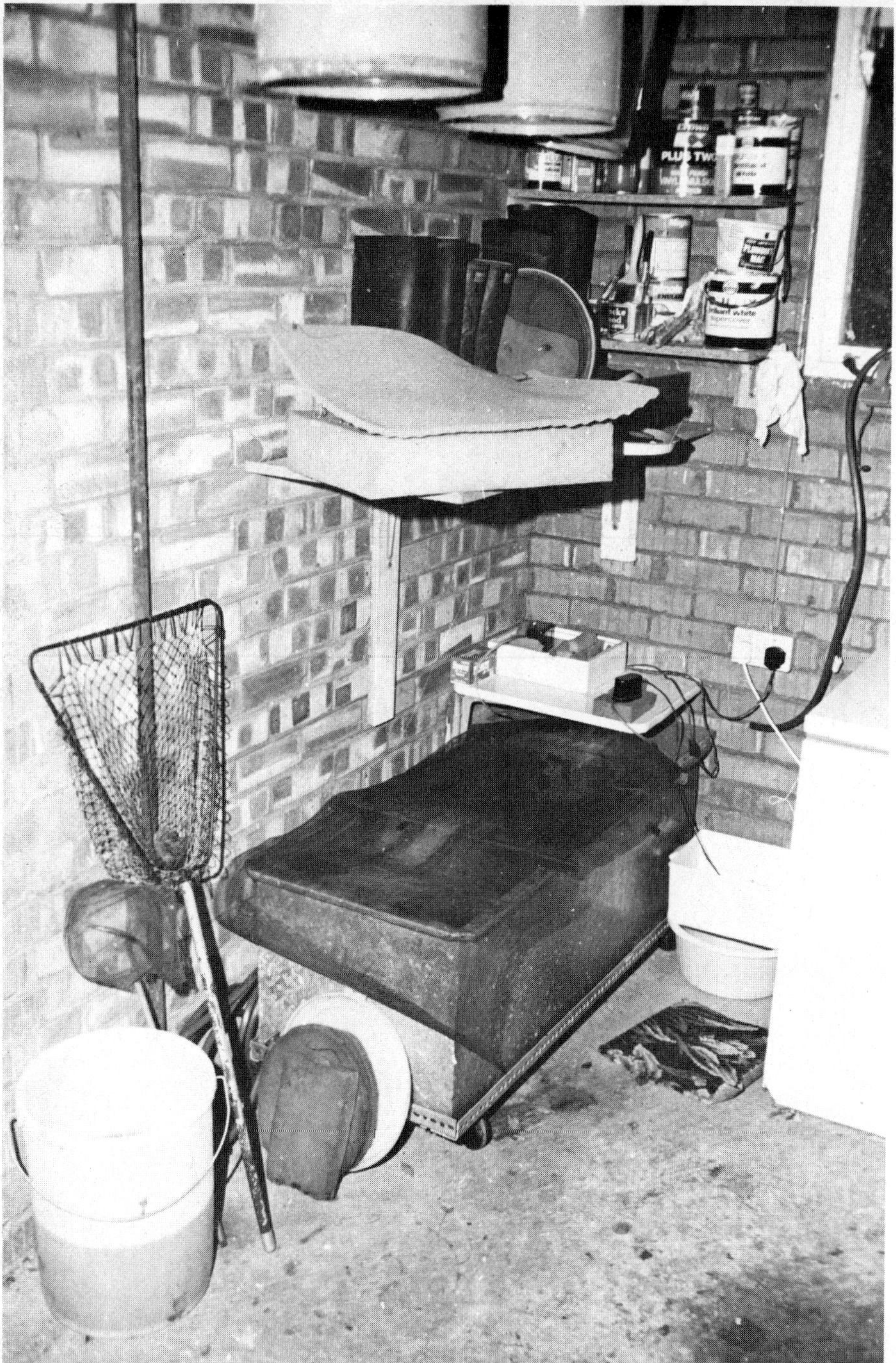
PLUS TWO

44

43 The author's bait corner of the garage, complete with livebait buckets, foam antisplash devices, snatching nets, freezer and so on.

44 The snatching net width just fits the width of the trough.

45

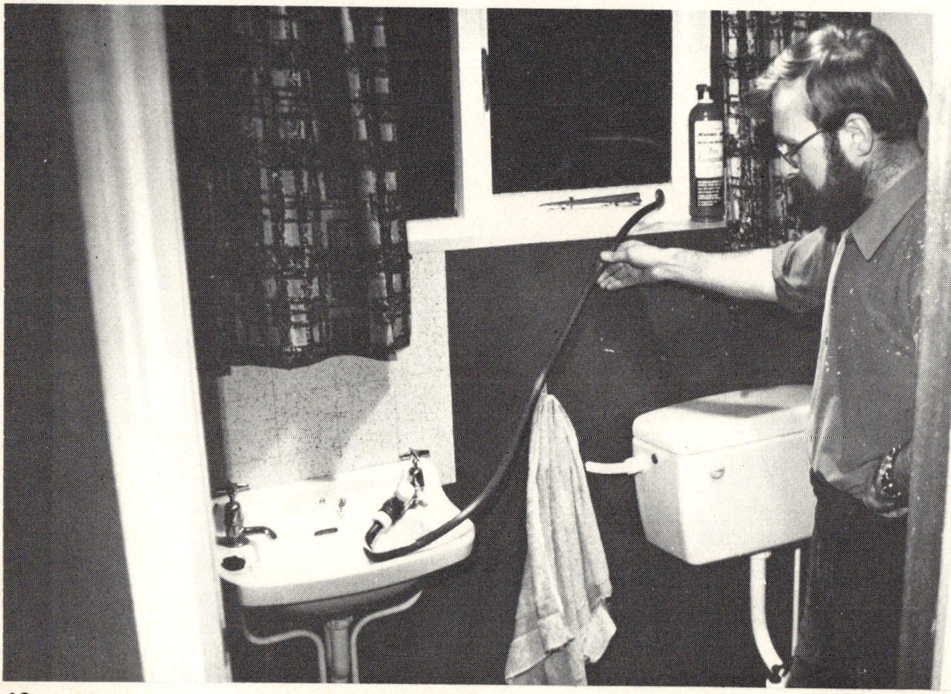

46

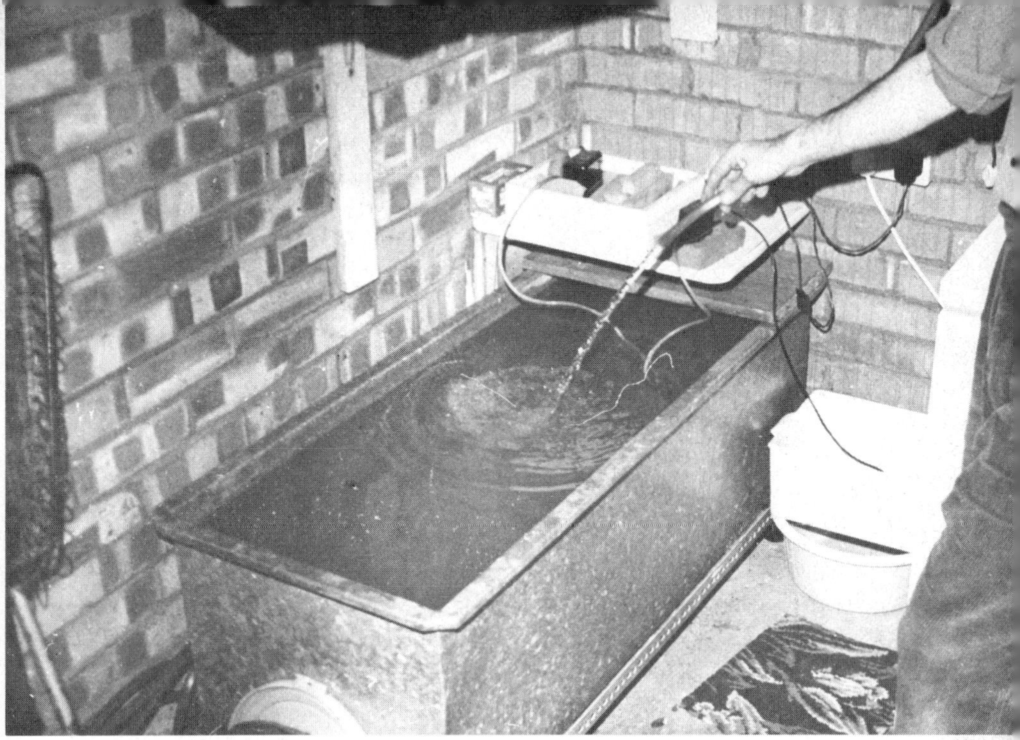

47

45 One sweep through the trough nets most of the contents with little fuss: except for dace, which are difficult to net.

46 The horse trough is filled from a bathroom sink via a permanently fitted pipe which goes through a hole drilled in the window frame, and similarly enters the garage.

47 The horse trough can be filled without much trouble.

48

49

50

48 Emptying the trough, a pipe is attached to the stopcock, and can be unrolled into the gutter.

49 The garden pond can be heated through cold spells, keeping it ice-free.

50 The pond heater floating in position.

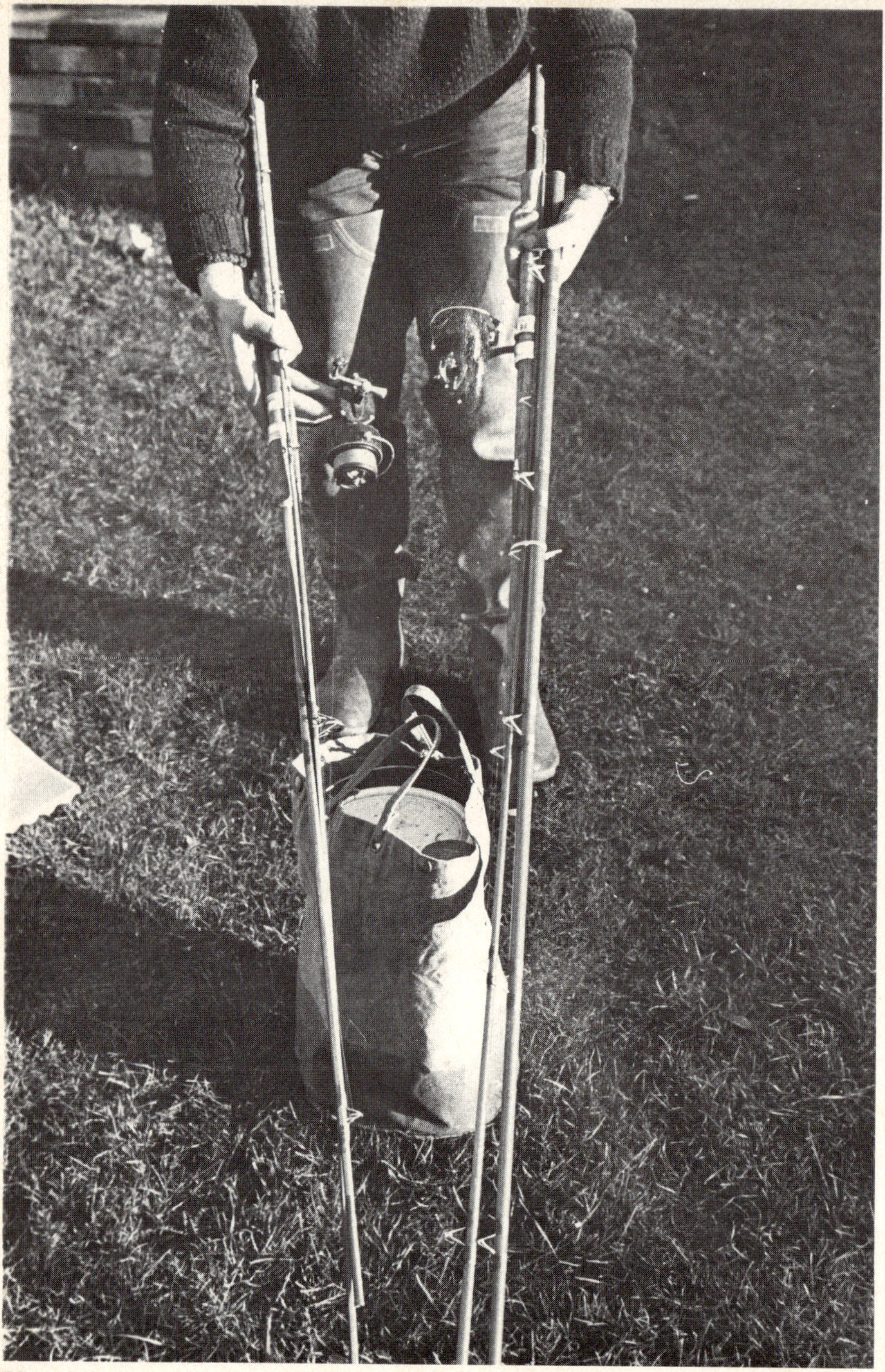

52

51 A complete set of 'snatching' tackle, with rods made up, is almost always carried by the author. One rod is a ten foot rod with a fitting for swing tip, but is usually set up to catch rudd. The other rod is a 14 foot Hardy's Fibretube, small float, 2lb line and size 20 hook.

52 A trap can also be used for catching livebait in some regions of the country: or in this case used to trap perch that have escaped amongst the goldfish!

53

54

53 Additional items in the equipment of the complete pike angler, a boat and outboard for carrying on a vehicle.

54 The van is filled prior to a session on a Fenland drain.

55 Ready for a pre-dawn start. Only the livebait bucket has to be loaded.

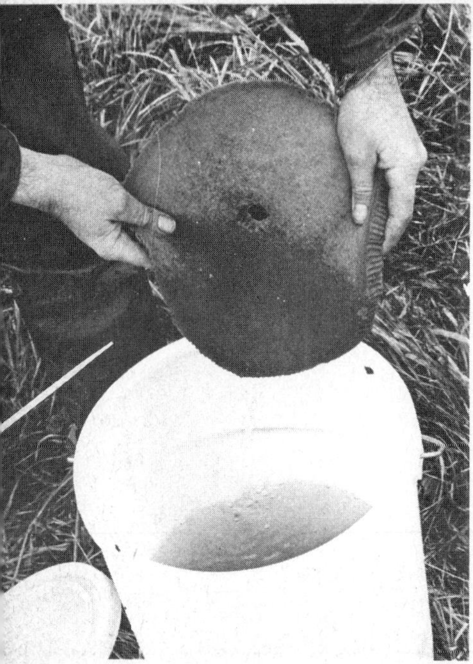

56

57

58

59

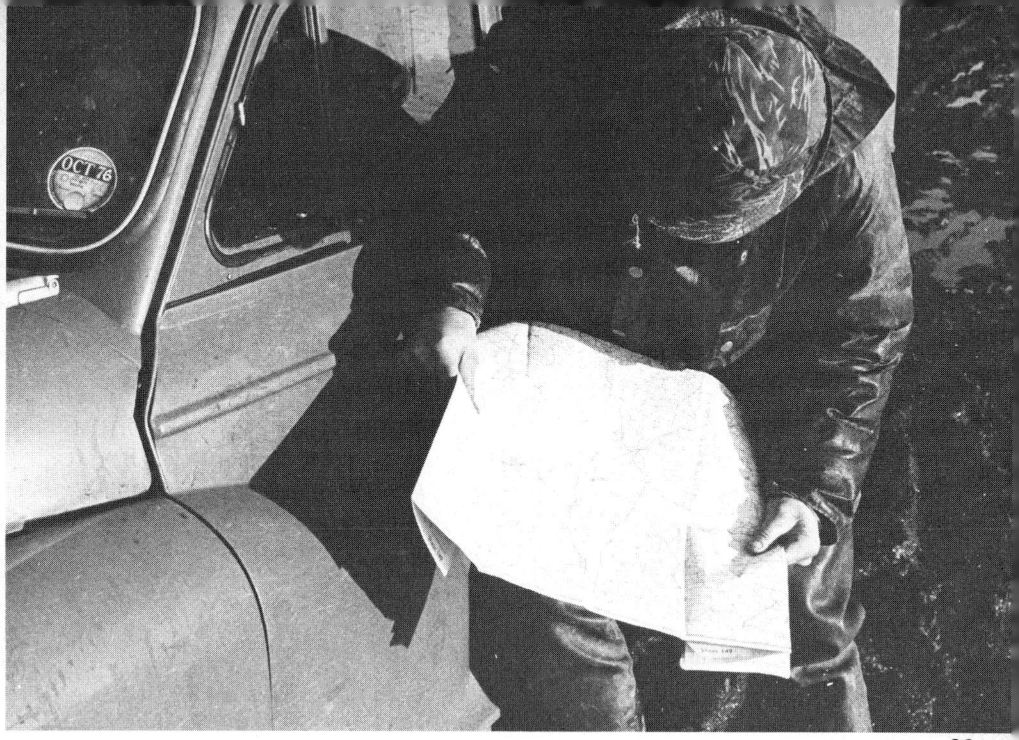

60

56 The livebait bucket is at least half-full and an anti-splash float is added.

57 There is a tight-fitting lid.

58 It is tied in position in the van.

59 The author usually braves the dirty dawns by wearing, even for driving, waders and an overlapping Barbour jacket.

60 A quick check of the map and away . . .

6

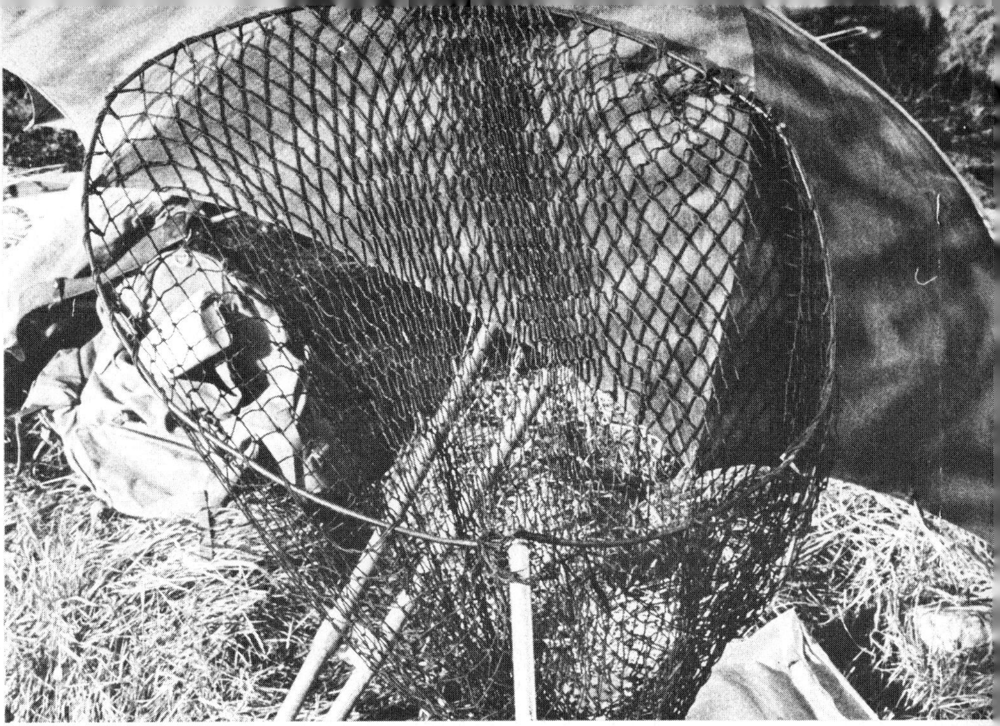

62

61 Author in walking kit: one holdall, one rucksack, and one bucket. Two miles is about the limit without a rest.

62 A base camp is established, but can be broken quickly if a move is decided upon.

63

64

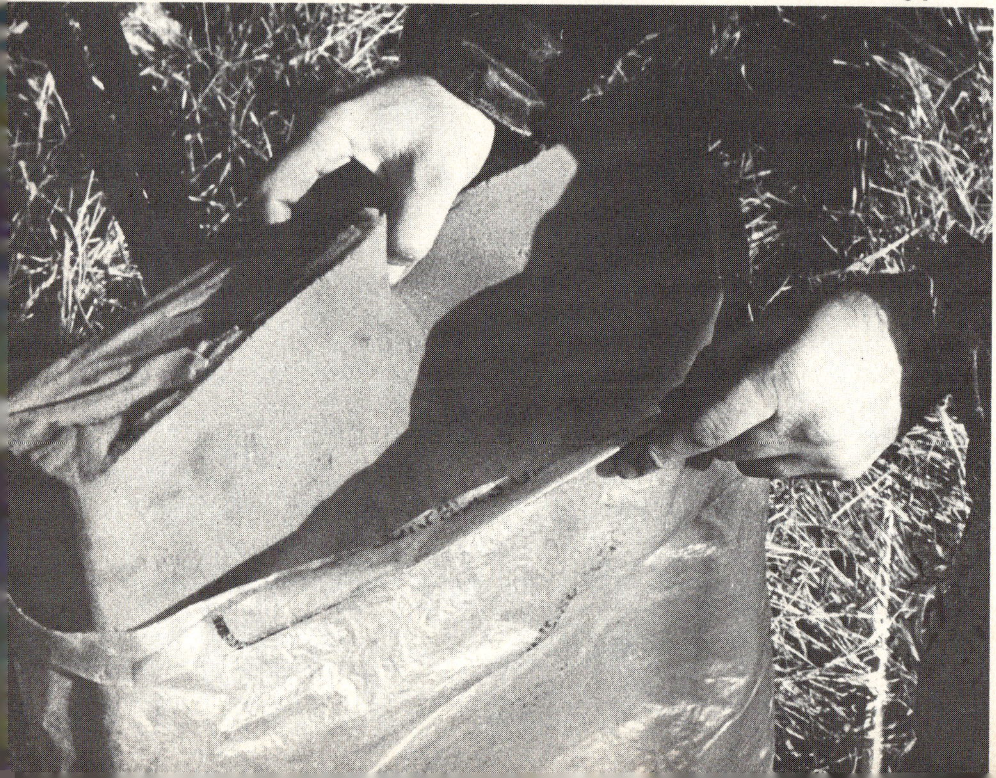

63 If it gets really cold a radiant heater is welcome.

64 And a soft seat to sit on. Fertilizer bags are very useful.

65 Tackling up.

67

66 A reel is clipped to the reel spool which was held in a pocket of the holdall. The reel is then attached to the rod, and the two rod pieces fitted together: no threading line through rings, tying knots etc.

67 Now all that is needed is a bait. Half a mackerel being prepared.

68

69

70

68 Frozen mackerel cut cleaner than this.

69 A sharp knife helps greatly.

70 A half mackerel mounted up and ready for use.

71

72

73

71 Air-injected herring is a bait that will settle softly on a weed-covered bottom.

72 Threading the trace through a herring when using the Ray Webb rig.

73 The Webb rig completed with the single treble about half way along the bait.

74

75

76

74 Similar rig but with the treble hook near the head, the trace again threaded.

75 The Fred J. Taylor rig with large single in the tail and two trebles along the flanks. An excellent design for casting.

76 Preparing the Steuart rig.

78

77 The Steuart rig complete. Large single in the tail and two trebles staggered down the two sides of the bait. The two diverging parts of the wire trace can be attached to the single hook.

78 Groundbaiting with a catapult.

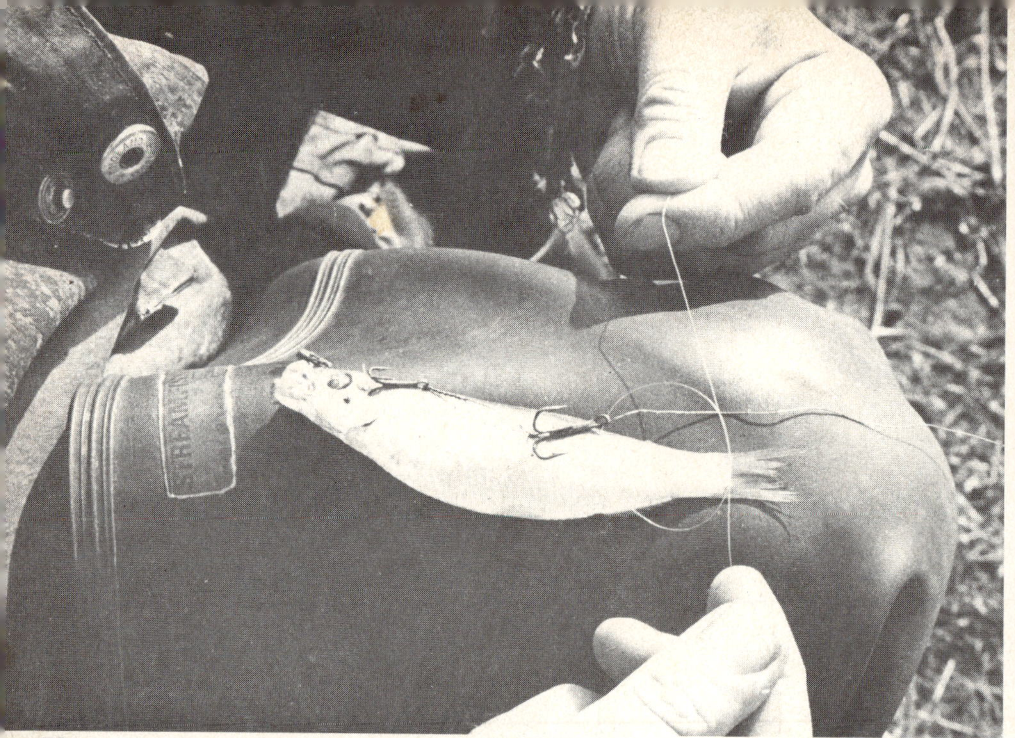

79

80

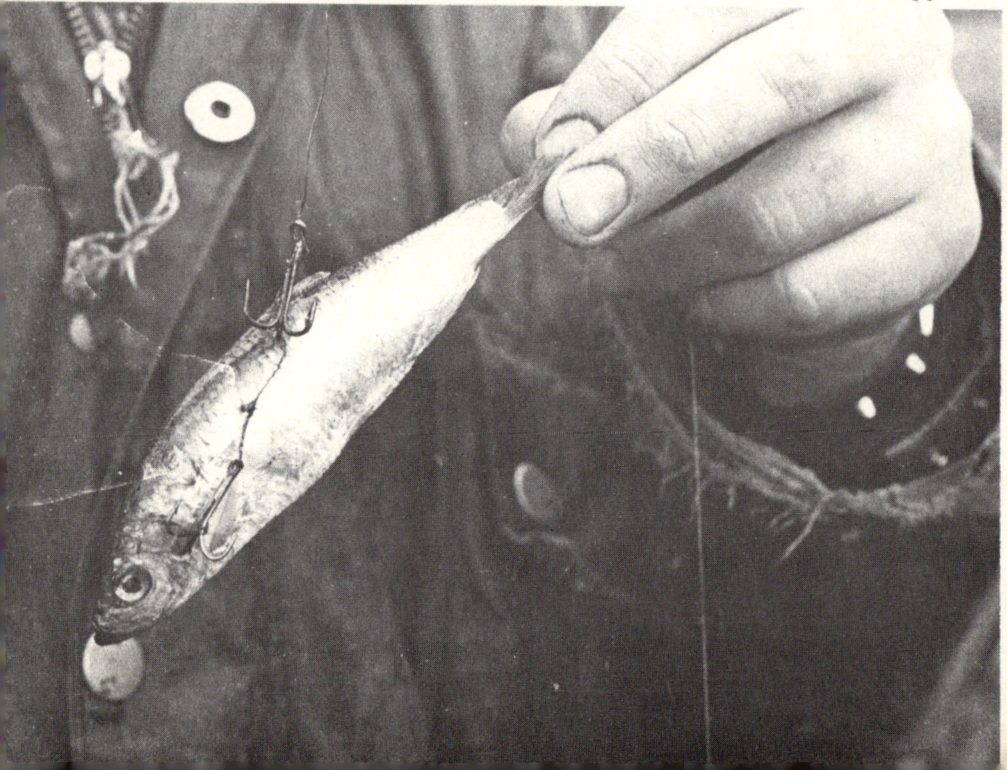

79 Sprats themselves make good deadbaits, but it is a help sometimes to tie them on the hooks. Sardines are too slippery for use.

80 Here a sprat is shown mounted for suspended deadbaiting.

81 The sliding float rig: a nylon stop knot, a bead, the sliding float, and a swan shot which can be above the trace for livebaiting or at the trace swivel for deadbaiting.

82

83

84

82 Paternoster rig consisting of an Arlesey Bomb, 6lb breaking strain paternoster line attached to the swivel eye of the snap tackle trace.

83 Sprat used to demonstrate hook arrangement for free-lined, ledgered livebait. A single treble, lip hooked, may also be used.

84 The similar rig for ledgered livebaiting using a sliding lead.

85

86

87

85 A dace livebait ready to go.

86 A sprat showing hooking arrangement for livebaiting with a snap tackle.

87 Choosing a livebait is cold on the hands in the depths of winter unless a small net is used.

89

88 For livebaiting a gentle swing, rather than a forceful cast, is often all that is needed.

89 Paternostered livebait tackle all ready.

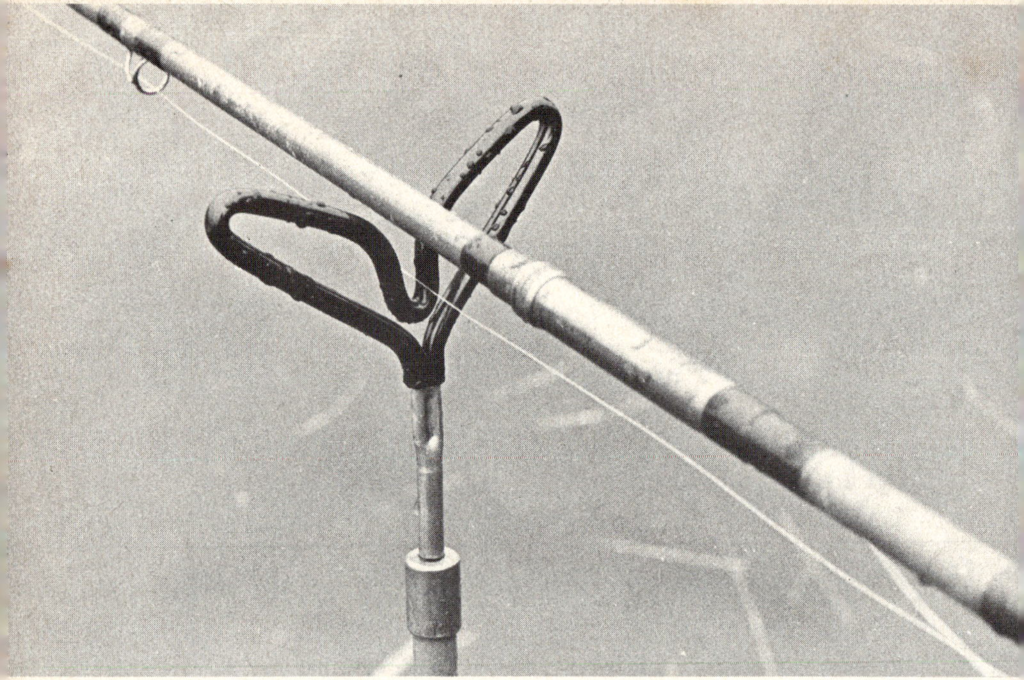

90

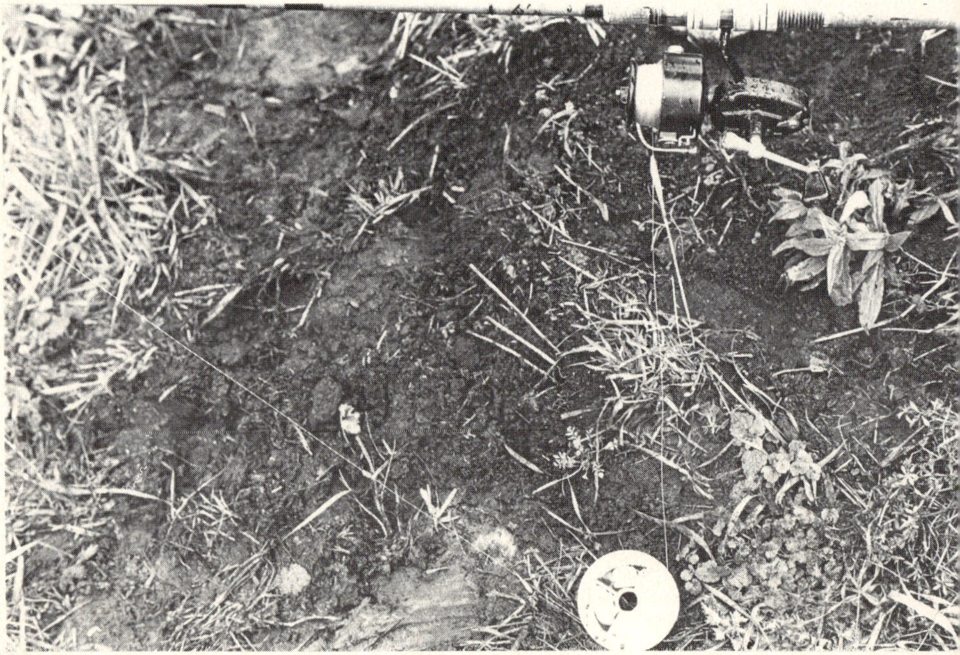

91

92

90 After casting, unless the rod is held, it should be placed in a rest of this type so that the line can run out freely after a take.

91 The pick-up should usually be left in the off position. An empty spool placed on the line at right angles to the reel to prevent wind blowing the line about, can be used as a stop and second indicator.

92 Silver paper or a fold of newspaper can serve instead of an empty spool.

93

94

95

93 A stick may be used in the absence of a more sophisticated bite indicator.

94 A roll of silver paper which stays on the line during the take: in windy weather it tends to spin during a take and tangles the line.

95 If a livebait weeds up on growing weed, remove it and recast.

96

97

98

96 A pike takes, the rod is picked up and all systems are checked for snags and tangles.

97 Line is paid out to the running pike, but not to a current. Hold the line against the pull of the current if there is one.

98 A small bait and a good snap tackle mean a strike as soon as the pike is running well. Do not wait for the 'second run'.

99

100

99 When the pike boils at the surface hold the rod low to make it dive again.

100 Holding a running fish on a short line early in the fight does no harm if either the clutch is set properly or the reel handle is free to rotate backwards.

101 The pike can be held away from bankside snags.

102

103

104

105

102 If a pike is difficult it can be pushed away from snags!

103 The landing net is sunk ready for the fish. The left elbow is on the end of the handle.

104 Head up and sliding steadily now . . .

105 Over the sunk net.

106

107

108

106 The pike is allowed to sink into the folds of the net, and pressure is taken off the rod at this point.

107 When lifting the pike out support the net frame either by holding it or the net itself.

108 Detail of the 29in diameter round landing net and frame. This is preferred by the author to large triangular nets.

109

110

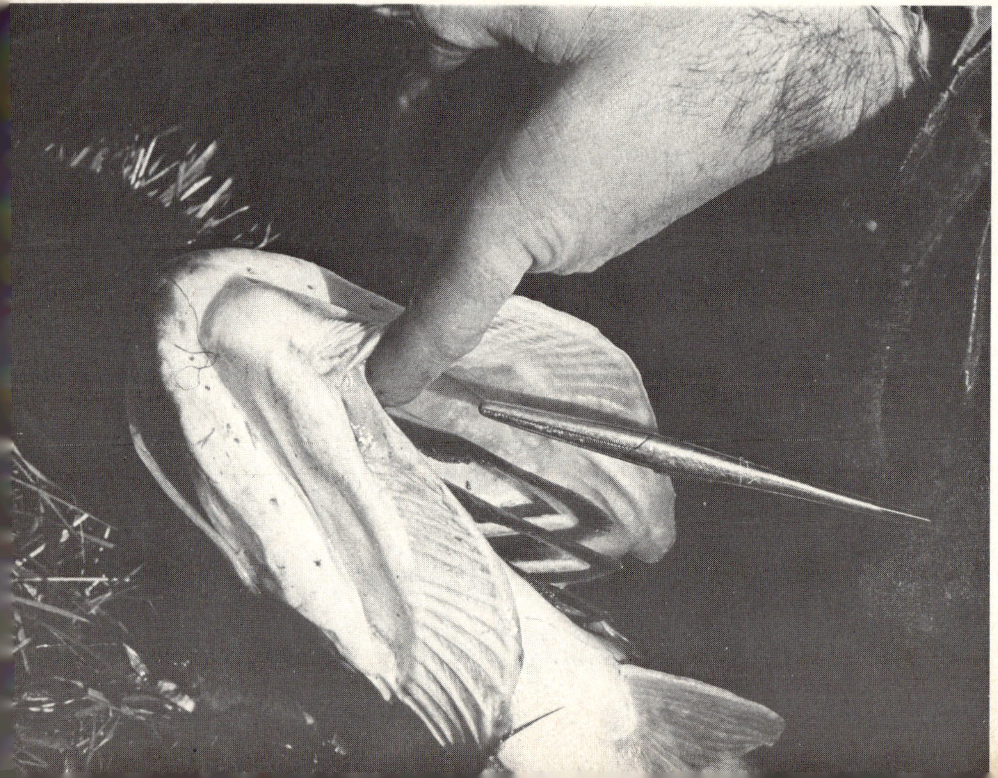

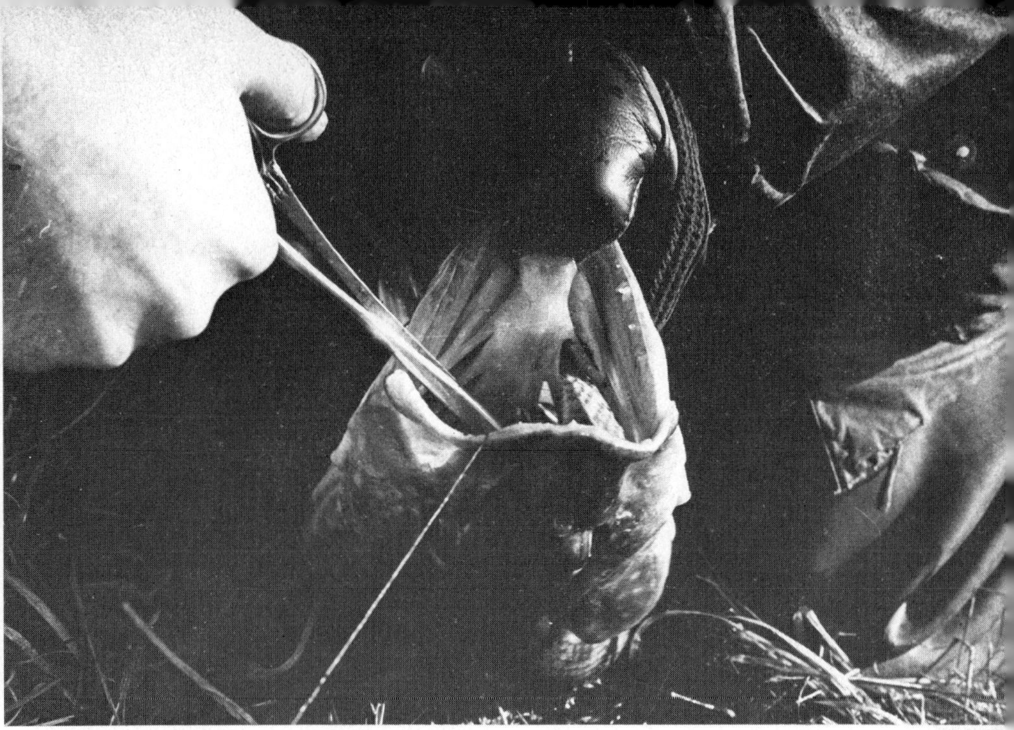

111

109 The left hand is held under the operculum (not in the gill filaments), the thumb pushes the pike's upper jaw forward, and forceps in the right hand are used to take the hooks out.

110 Showing the position for one or two fingers for the unhooking hold in the left hand.

111 The best unhooking method of all is to use a glove as shown, when the pike easily opens its mouth.

113

112 Time for a break in the base camp. Plenty of food is needed for a full winter's day of piking.

113 If a gag is used, though they seem hardly necessary these days, some of the strength of the gag should be taken in the left hand.

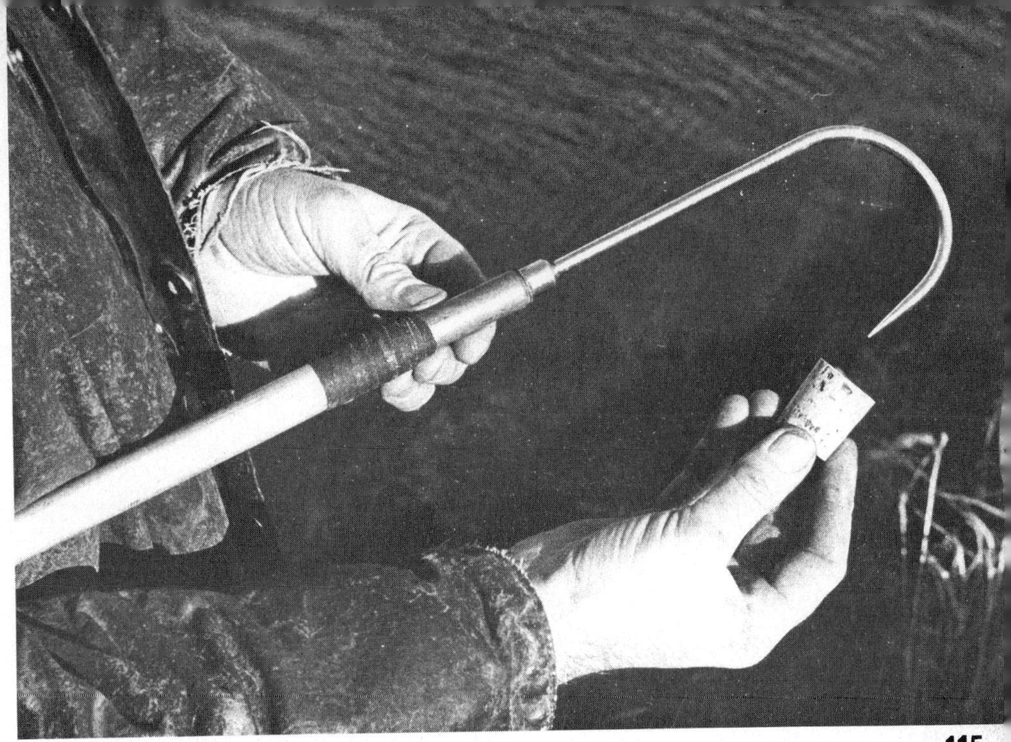

114 When gaffing a pike the point of the gaff should go in the very point of the jaw, not into the gills, or anywhere else for that matter.

115 On the bank, a gaff point should be protected with a cork. Round bend gaffs are less useful than V-shaped ones.

116

117

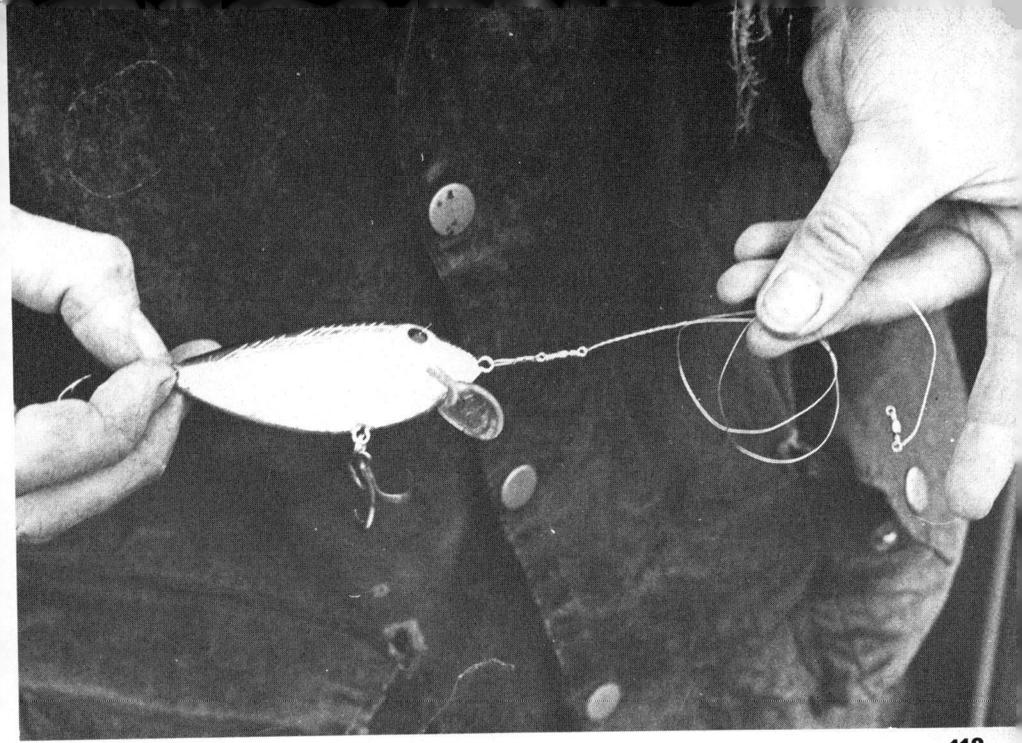

118

116 The fish is slipped into the weighing net. Muslin is kinder on the fish than netting.

117 Weighed like this, the fish rarely flaps.

118 Now for spinning. The simple wire trace with swivel and link swivel is shown.

119

120

119 The reel, as always, should have the spool filled to the lip.

120 This Gudebrod Sniper, in yellow, is a favourite for the shallow fen drains and rivers.

121 Although it can be worked very shallow it does pick up weed. Remove any weed before recasting.

122

123

124

125

122 Spinning stance: rod tip low, arms low, rod not quite pointing at the lure.

123 Slow wobblers are often engulfed and slack line takes are common.

124 Nearly ready.

125 Drawing the fish to the left hand. This method of landing is dangerous when lure fishing.

127

126 The pike is gripped as shown. This method of landing is not good for fish over 8 pounds. It's a lazy technique suitable for small pike.

127 The same hold can be used again for unhooking. But beware treble hooks.

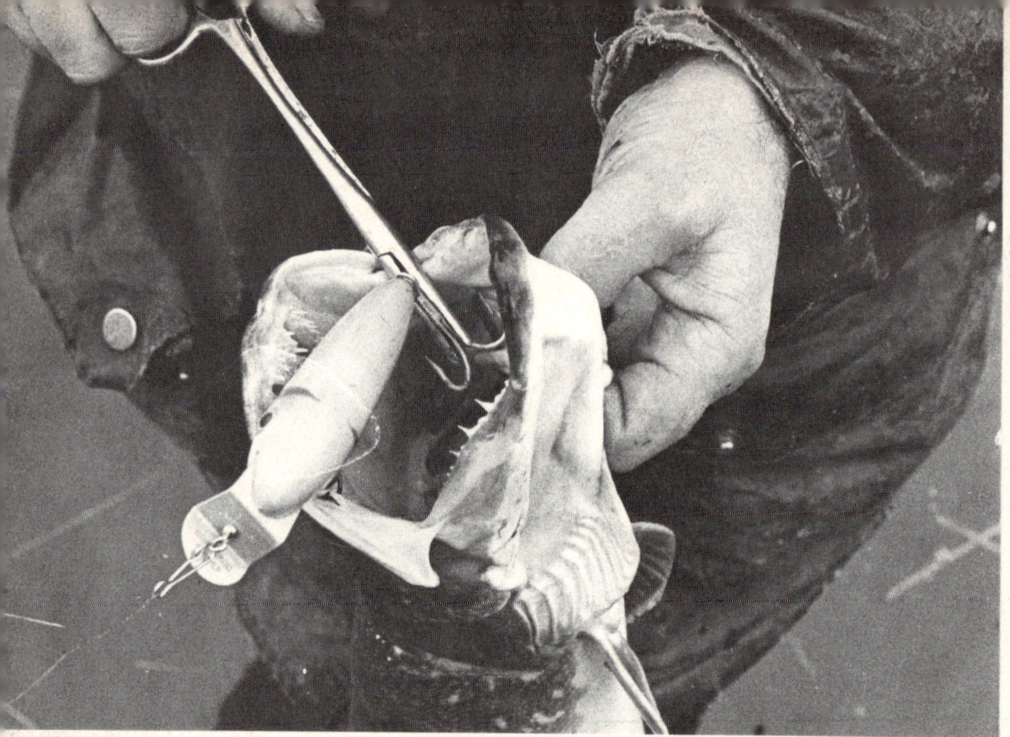

128

129

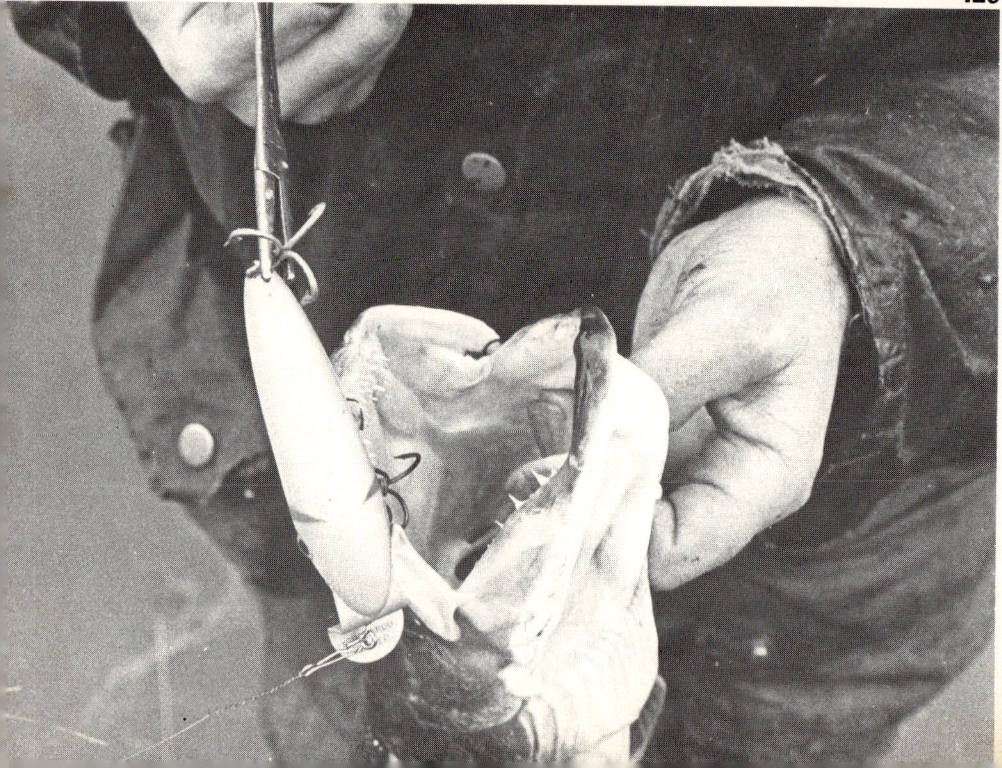

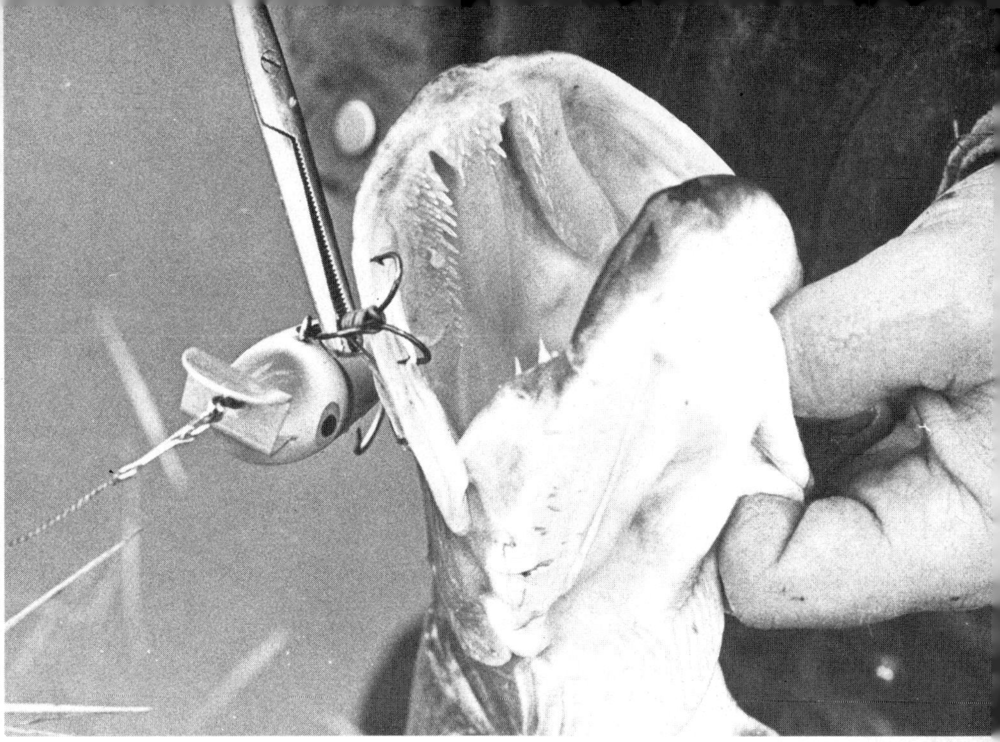

130

128 The bottom treble is freed first.

129 Only the top treble remaining.

130 And now the top treble; the hook hold is well shown.

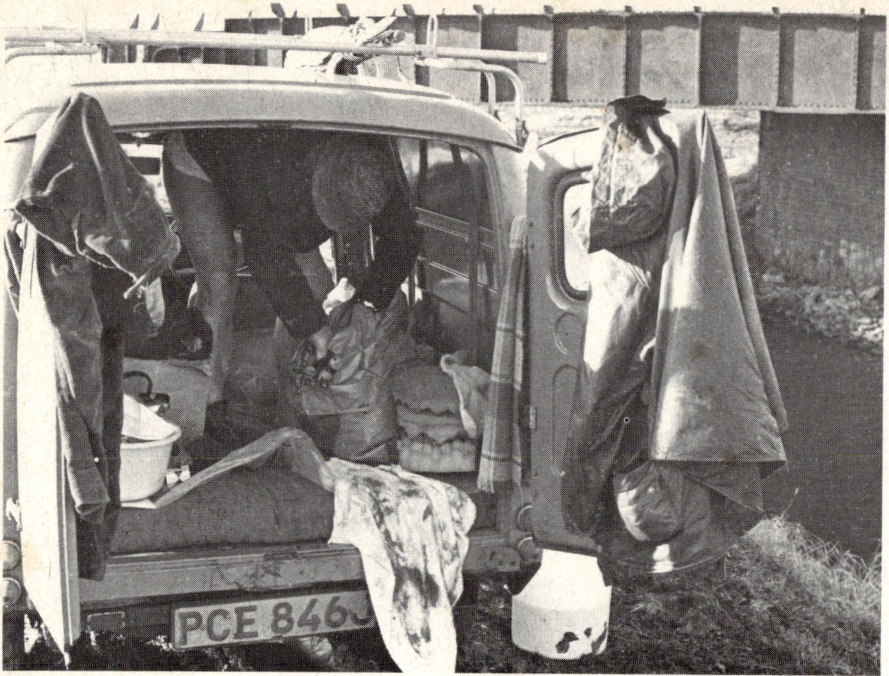

131

132

133

131 Accidents will happen. Always carry a spare bag full of old clothes.

132 Another fish on the way to the net.

133 At the end of the day an excellent bag of fish averaging 6 pounds each.

134

135

136

134 Trimming a mackerel tail fin to get extra yards on a long cast.

135 Laying back the rod to test for snags on the backcast. A Lea Valley gravel pit.

136 Wumph. The rod comes through at about seventy degrees from the horizontal.

137

138

139

137 Near the end of the main punch.

138 At the end of the cast the rod tip tends to dive to the water, but try to prevent this.

139 Placing the rod in the rests to await a deadbait run.

140

141

142

140 Sitting back with binoculars to watch the float; and to watch other bankside activities.

141 The netsman should get into position early.

142 Winding up to a pike before striking.

143

144

143 Beginning of the strike; on the way up.

144 The moment of impact. If the line has been taken up correctly there is no need to take dozens of steps backwards.

145 Ray Webb calmly netting a good fish for the author.

147

146 Another good battle on. The strength of the Olivers' stepped-up carp rod is well seen here.

147 This time a small one, wallowing just before landing.

149

148 Sliding the fish to the left hand.

149 The fish swerves away again.

151

152

150 This fish gives a spirited performance.

151 Another small but perfectly shaped and fit pike.

152 The author, back in the Fenlands.

The pictures you have seen show how an expert tackles Pike fishing. Now go back to the beginning of the book and carefully study each sequence again. Compare the expert's approach with your own, and select what you think will improve your own fishing. Practise your new ideas — and then try to improve on them.

Always remember that an expert is the angler who constantly analyses his own styles, improves on what he is doing — and then practises until he is perfect.